D1404696

21st Century
Basic Skills
Library

KIDS CAN MAKE MANNERS COUNT
BE ON TIME!

by Katie Marsico

Cherry Lake Publishing • Ann Arbor, Michigan

3

CHERRY
LAKE
Publishing

Published in the United States of America
by Cherry Lake Publishing
Ann Arbor, Michigan
www.cherrylakepublishing.com

Content Adviser: Tonia Bock, PhD, Associate Professor of Psychology,
St. Thomas University, St. Paul, Minnesota

Photo Credits: Cover and pages 1, 4, 6, 8, 10, 12, and 20,
©Keri Langlois; page 14, ©Anneka/Shutterstock, Inc.;
page 16, ©Andrey Savin/Shutterstock, Inc.; page 18,
©cappi thompson/Shutterstock, Inc.

Library of Congress Cataloging-in-Publication Data
Marsico, Katie, 1980–
  Be on time! / by Katie Marsico.
     p. cm.—(21st century basic skills library) (Kids can make
manners count)
  Includes bibliographical references and index.
  ISBN 978-1-61080-435-6 (lib. bdg.)—ISBN 978-1-61080-522-3 (e-book)—
ISBN 978-1-61080-609-1 (pbk.)
 1. Time perception. 2. Self-management (Psychology) 3. Children—
Conduct of life. I. Title.
  BF468.M36 2013
  395.1'22—dc23
                                                        2012001706

Cherry Lake Publishing would like to acknowledge
the work of The Partnership for 21st Century Skills.
Please visit www.21stcenturyskills.org for more information.

Printed in the United States of America
Corporate Graphics Inc.
July 2012
CLFA11

TABLE OF CONTENTS

A Soccer Problem

Anna was the best player on her soccer team.

Yet she was usually late to games on Saturdays.

This was because she never woke up on time.

Anna's team kept losing games.

Coach Tim was sad and angry.
He knew Anna could help the
team win.

She wasn't always there when
she was needed, though.

Making Manners Work

Anna loved soccer.

She also enjoyed sleeping late on Saturdays.

Coach Tim decided to talk to her. He had a **solution** to this problem.

Anna listened to Coach Tim. He said it was important to be on time.

Being on time was an example of having good **manners**.

Anna was never **tardy** for class.

She was in her seat when the bell rang.

Anna was even on time for soccer practice.

Always on Time

Coach Tim told Anna that she always needed to be on time.

He said it was **rude** to make other people wait. They may have other things to do. Waiting can keep them from doing these things.

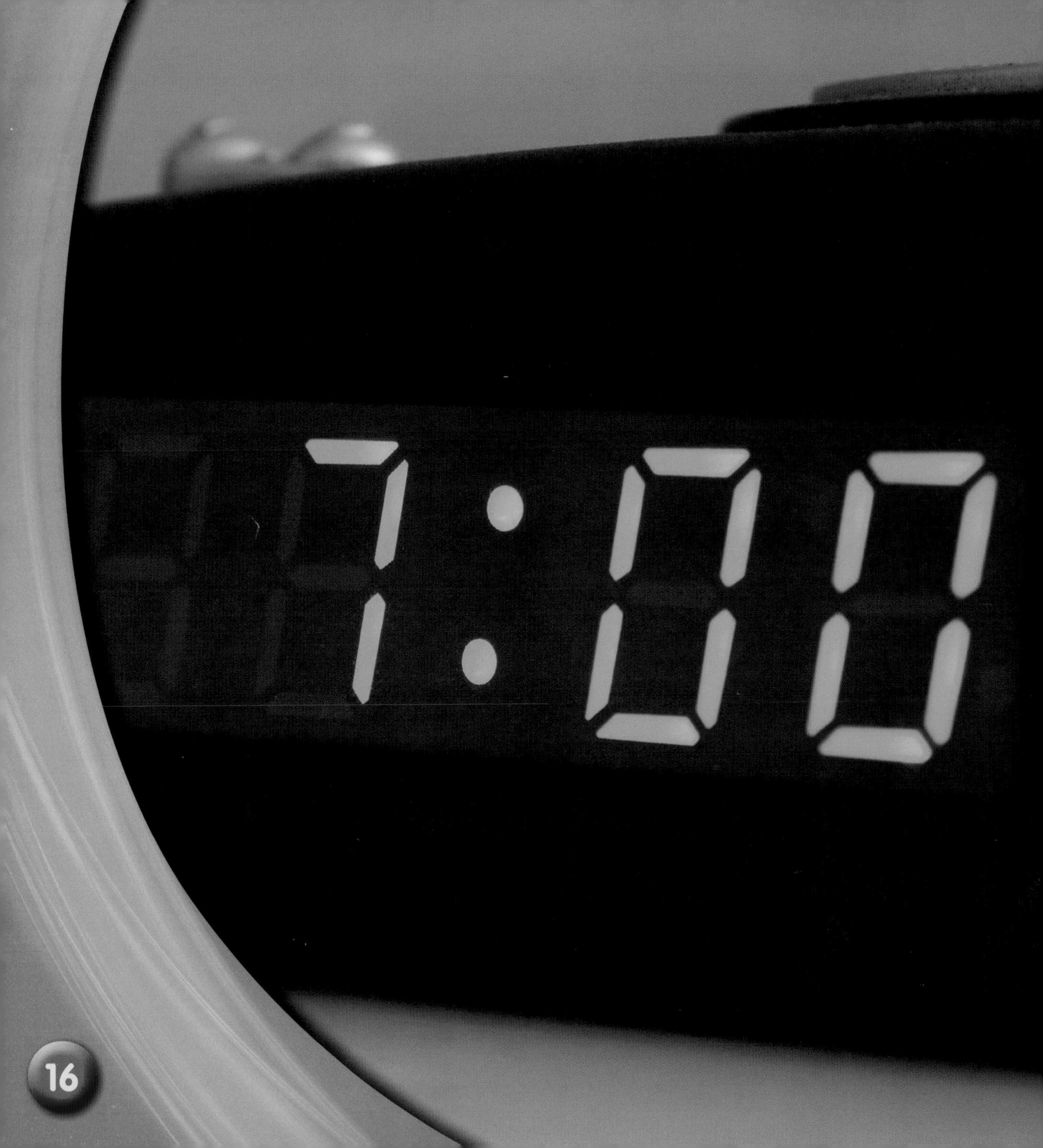
7:00

Coach Tim said Anna should use an alarm clock. It would wake her up on Saturdays.

He told her to go to bed earlier on Fridays, too. Then she would get plenty of sleep.

Anna also made a **schedule** for Saturday mornings.

She set aside time to shower and eat a healthy breakfast.

Soon Anna was hardly ever late.

She played more often on Saturdays. Her team started winning games.

Anna was showing good manners and scoring goals!

Find Out More

BOOK

Marshall, Shelley, and Ben Mahan (illustrator). *Molly the Great Misses the Bus: A Book About Being on Time.* Berkeley Heights, NJ: Enslow Publishers, 2010.

WEB SITE

U.S. Department of Health and Human Services— Building Blocks: Manners Quiz

www.bblocks.samhsa.gov/family/activities/quizzes/manners.aspx

Take a fun online quiz to test how much you know about manners!

Glossary

manners (MA-nurz) behavior that is kind and polite

rude (ROOD) having bad manners

schedule (SKEJ-ool) a plan for doing something at a certain date and time

solution (suh-LOO-shuhn) an answer to a problem

tardy (TAR-dee) late

Home and School Connection

Use this list of words from the book to help your child become a better reader. Word games and writing activities can help beginning readers reinforce literacy skills.

a	decided	healthy	of	shower	to
alarm	do	help	often	showing	told
also	doing	her	on	sleep	too
always	earlier	important	other	sleeping	up
an	eat	in	people	soccer	use
and	enjoyed	it	played	solution	usually
angry	even	keep	player	soon	wait
Anna	ever	kept	plenty	started	waiting
Anna's	example	knew	practice	talk	wake
aside	for	late	problem	tardy	was
be	Fridays	listened	rang	team	wasn't
bed	from	losing	rude	that	when
because	games	loved	sad	the	win
being	get	made	said	them	winning
bell	go	make	Saturday	then	woke
best	goals	making	Saturdays	there	work
breakfast	good	manners	schedule	these	would
can	had	may	scoring	things	yet
class	hardly	more	seat	this	
clock	have	mornings	set	though	
coach	having	needed	she	Tim	
could	he	never	should	time	

23

Index

About the Author

Katie Marsico is an author of children's and young-adult reference books. She lives outside of Chicago, Illinois, with her husband and children.